SPORTS SUPERSTARS

NAOMI OSAKA

BY GOLRIZ GOLKAR

TORQUE

BELLWETHER MEDIA · MINNEAPOLIS, MN

Torque brims with excitement perfect for thrill-seekers of all kinds. Discover daring survival skills, explore uncharted worlds, and marvel at mighty engines and extreme sports. In *Torque* books, anything can happen. Are you ready?

This edition first published in 2024 by Bellwether Media, Inc.

No part of this publication may be reproduced in whole or in part without written permission of the publisher. For information regarding permission, write to Bellwether Media, Inc., Attention: Permissions Department, 6012 Blue Circle Drive, Minnetonka, MN 55343.

Library of Congress Cataloging-in-Publication Data

LC record for Naomi Osaka available at: https://lccn.loc.gov/2023040014

Text copyright © 2024 by Bellwether Media, Inc. TORQUE and associated logos are trademarks and/or registered trademarks of Bellwether Media, Inc.

Editor: Rebecca Sabelko   Designer: Gabriel Hilger

Printed in the United States of America, North Mankato, MN.

TABLE OF CONTENTS

A TENNIS STAR IS BORN	4
WHO IS NAOMI OSAKA?	6
A YOUNG TALENT	8
A TENNIS CHAMPION	12
A BRIGHT FUTURE	20
GLOSSARY	22
TO LEARN MORE	23
INDEX	24

A TENNIS STAR IS BORN

It is the 2018 U.S. Open women's **finals**. Naomi Osaka is playing against tennis superstar Serena Williams. Osaka has already won the first **set** of the **match**. She leads in the second set.

Osaka slams the ball over the net. Williams tries to return the ball. But she hits it outside the court. Osaka wins her first **Grand Slam**!

2018 U.S. OPEN CHAMPION

Making History

Osaka's win at the U.S. Open made her the first Japanese tennis player to win a Grand Slam.

WHO IS NAOMI OSAKA?

Naomi Osaka is a **professional** tennis player. She has won many Grand Slams. She is known for her skill and focus during matches. They have made her one of the top women's tennis players in the world.

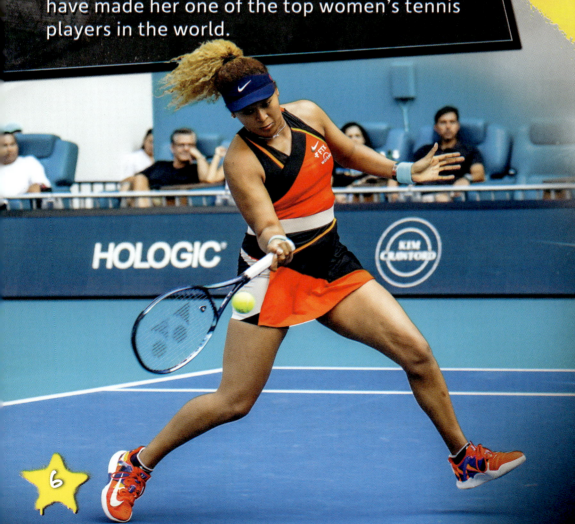

NAOMI OSAKA

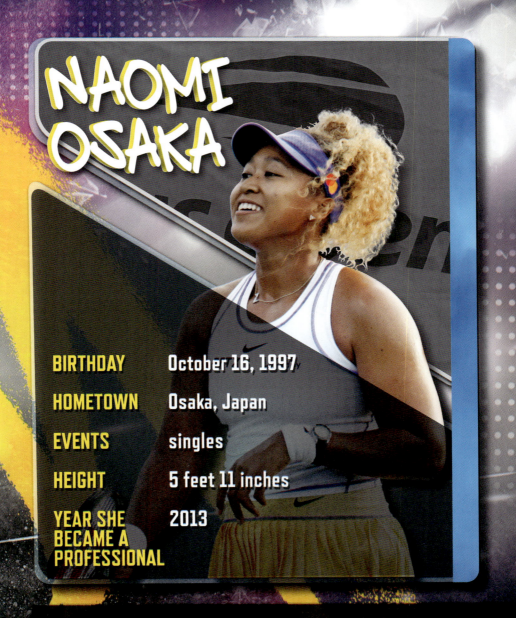

BIRTHDAY	October 16, 1997
HOMETOWN	Osaka, Japan
EVENTS	singles
HEIGHT	5 feet 11 inches
YEAR SHE BECAME A PROFESSIONAL	2013

She is also interested in fashion. She works with many brands. They include Nike and Levi's. She also supports gender and racial equality.

A YOUNG TALENT

Osaka was born in Japan. She moved to New York with her family at age 3. Her father taught her sister and her to play tennis.

OSAKA WITH HER FATHER

OSAKA WITH HER PARENTS AND COACH

The family moved to Florida when Osaka was around 9 years old. She focused on her training. She practiced with her father during the day. She studied at night.

Osaka became a professional tennis player in 2013. She joined the **Women's Tennis Association** (WTA). She grew up in the United States. But she chose to play for Japan. She made it to the finals of many small **tournaments**.

She was one of the final 32 players at three Grand Slam tournaments in 2016. The WTA named her Newcomer of the Year!

2016 FRENCH OPEN

Super Serve

Osaka hit a 125-mile-per-hour (201-kilometer-per-hour) serve at the 2016 U.S. Open. It was one of the fastest serves recorded for a female tennis player.

FAVORITES

SINGER	FOOD	ANIMAL	HOBBY
Beyoncé	green tea ice cream	dogs	video games

A TENNIS CHAMPION

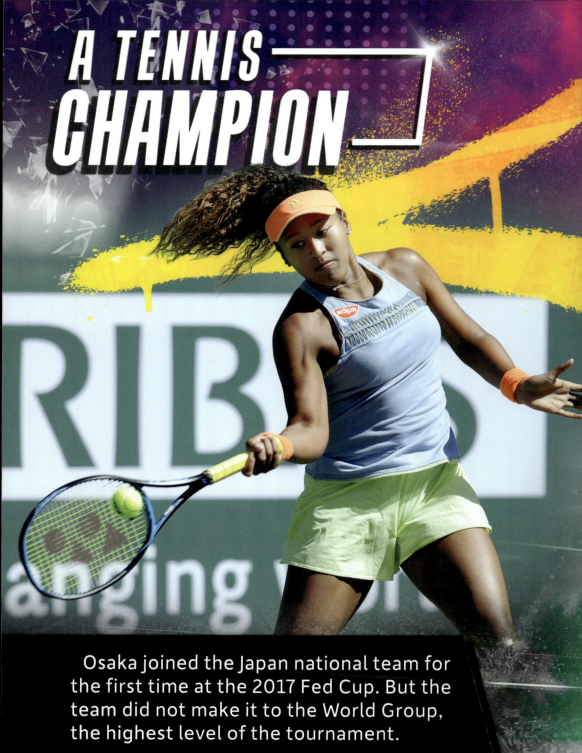

Osaka joined the Japan national team for the first time at the 2017 Fed Cup. But the team did not make it to the World Group, the highest level of the tournament.

She won her first WTA tournament in March of 2018. It was at the BNP Paribas Open. She beat the world's highest-ranked female tennis player.

2018 BNP PARIBAS OPEN CHAMPION

2018 U.S. OPEN

Osaka played in the U.S. Open six months later. It was her first Grand Slam final. She won the tournament!

She won her second Grand Slam at the 2019 Australian Open. She became the number one female tennis player in the world. She became the first Asian player to reach the number one spot!

Osaka won her second U.S. Open in 2020. Many people also noticed her for her **activism**. She wore masks with the names of Black people who had died from **racism** in the U.S.

The Associated Press named her Female Athlete of the Year. She won the award for playing well and her activism.

2020 U.S. OPEN CHAMPION

TROPHY SHELF

2-time Australian Open champion

2-time U.S. Open champion

WTA Newcomer of the Year

AP Female Athlete of the Year

17

Osaka played in the 2021 Australian Open. It became her fourth Grand Slam title.

She also played at the Tokyo **Summer Olympics**. She played for the Japan national team. She was chosen to light the torch at the Opening Ceremony. She played her best. But she did not win a medal.

2021 AUSTRALIAN OPEN CHAMPION

TIMELINE

— 2013 —
Osaka becomes a professional tennis player

— 2016 —
Osaka reaches her first WTA final and is named WTA Newcomer of the Year

— 2018 —
Osaka wins her first Grand Slam title at the U.S. Open

18

2020 TOKYO SUMMER OLYMPICS

— 2019 —
Osaka wins her second Grand Slam title at the Australian Open

— 2020 —
Osaka wins her third Grand Slam title at the U.S. Open

— 2021 —
Osaka wins her fourth Grand Slam title at the Australian Open

A BRIGHT FUTURE

Osaka did not play well after the Tokyo Olympics. She needed to care for her **mental health**. She took time off to get well. She focused on other business projects.

Play Academy

Osaka co-founded Play Academy in 2020. It gives money to sports groups to support girls.

She also took time off in 2023 after having a baby. But she plans to play in the near future. She hopes to win more titles!

GLOSSARY

activism—supporting strong actions in favor of a social cause

finals—the championship series of a sports tournament

Grand Slam—one of the four most important professional tennis tournaments of the year; the Grand Slam tournaments are the Australian Open, the French Open, Wimbledon, and the U.S. Open.

match—a series of games between tennis players

mental health—the way people think and feel about themselves and the world around them

professional—related to a player, team, or coach who makes money from a sport

racism—when people are treated unfairly because of their skin color or background

set—a unit of scoring in tennis; a player must win two out of three or three out of five sets to win a match.

Summer Olympics—a worldwide summer sports contest held in a different country every four years

tournaments—series of games in which several teams or players try to win championships

Women's Tennis Association—a professional tennis league; the Women's Tennis Association is often called the WTA.

TO LEARN MORE

AT THE LIBRARY

Scarbrough, Mary Hertz. *Naomi Osaka.* Greensboro, N.C.: Rourke Educational Media, 2021.

Scheff, Matt. *Naomi Osaka: Tennis Star.* Lake Elmo, Minn.: Focus Readers, 2020.

Youssef, Jagger. *Naomi Osaka.* New York, N.Y.: Gareth Stevens Publishing, 2024.

ON THE WEB

Factsurfer.com gives you a safe, fun way to find more information.

1. Go to www.factsurfer.com

2. Enter "Naomi Osaka" into the search box and click 🔍.

3. Select your book cover to see a list of related content.

INDEX

activism, 16
Australian Open, 14, 15, 18
awards, 4, 5, 10, 13, 14, 16, 17, 18
BNP Paribas Open, 13
childhood, 8, 9, 10
equality, 7
family, 8, 9, 21
fashion, 7
favorites, 11
Fed Cup, 12
Female Athlete of the Year, 16
finals, 4, 10, 14
Florida, 9
future, 21
Grand Slam, 4, 5, 6, 10, 14, 18
Japan, 5, 8, 10, 12, 18

map, 15
masks, 16
mental health, 20
New York, 8
Newcomer of the Year, 10
Play Academy, 21
profile, 7
racism, 16
serve, 11
Summer Olympics, 18, 19, 20
timeline, 18–19
tournaments, 10, 12, 13, 14
trophy shelf, 17
U.S. Open, 4, 5, 11, 14, 16, 17
Women's Tennis Association, 10, 13

The images in this book are reproduced through the courtesy of: MediaPunch/ AP Images/ AP Newsroom, front cover; Leonard Zhukovsky, pp. 3, 6, 7 (U.S. Open flag); lev radin, pp. 4, 4-5, 15 (U.S. Open stadium); Santiago Mejia/ AP Images/ AP Newsroom, p. 7 (Naomi Osaka); Aflo Co. Ltd./ Alamy, p. 8; Mami Nagaoki/ AP Images/ AP Newsroom, p. 9; Christophe Ena/ AP Images/ AP Newsroom, p. 10; Storms Meida Group/ Alamy, p. 11 (Naomi Osaka); Everett Collection Inc/ Alamy, p. 11 (Beyoncé); Anna_Pustynnikova, p. 11 (green tea ice cream); Csanad Kiss, p. 11 (dogs); Diego Thomazini, p. 11 (video game controllers); John Cordes/ Icon Sportswire/ AP Images/ AP Newsroom, p. 12; Mal Taam/ AP Images/ AP Newsroom, p. 13; Cynthia Lum/ Icon Sportswire/ AP Images/ AP Newsroom, p. 14; show999, p. 15 (Tokyo Olympics stadium); Neale Cousland, p. 15 (Australian Open stadium); Aaron Favila/ AP Images/ AP Newsroom, p. 15 (Naomi Osaka); Frank Franklin/ AP Images/ AP Newsroom, p. 16; Seth Wenig/ AP Images/ AP Newsroom, p. 17; Andy Brownbill/ AP Images/ AP Newsroom, p. 18 (2021 Australian Open champion); Kydlp Kyodo/ AP Images/ AP Newsroom, pp. 18-19; Simon Bruty/ AP Images/ AP Newsroom, p. 19 (2020 Grand Slam); Kyodo News/ Contributor/ Getty Images, p. 20; Frank Franklin II/ AP Newsroom, p. 21; YES Market Media, p. 23.